T0209313

FEMININITY

A Collection of Poems

Bianca Irene

WESTBOW
P R E S S®
A DIVISION OF THOMAS NELSON
& ZONDERVAN

WestBow Press books may be ordered through booksellers or by contacting:

WestBow Press
A Division of Thomas Nelson & Zondervan
1663 Liberty Drive
Bloomington, IN 47403
www.westbowpress.com
844-714-3454

ISBN: 979-8-3850-0479-9 (sc)
ISBN: 979-8-3850-0472-0 (e)

Library of Congress Control Number: 2023914767

Print information available on the last page.

WestBow Press rev. date: 09/26/2023

For my daughter,
Sofia Joy.

For the Reader

I wrote this book from the pit of my stomach,
the brokenness of my spirit,
and the joy of my salvation.

Please do not hold back
in shedding your tears,
crying out to God, and
allowing Him to touch your heart.

My prayer for you is that you would
see Jesus through the broken parts of me
and know that He sees you and loves you
in the depths of your brokenness.

Contents

THE SEARCH

THE DISCOVERY

THE SEARCH

Refuge

Can I speak?
Can I breathe?
Can I remove this facade,
convinced it's better kept on,
and release what's underneath?

I feel the waves crash against me
with determined attempts
to tear this temple down.
My back has grown sore
from the weight of patience.
My eyes memorized the details
of the tiles on my bathroom floor.

It used to be the place
that cradled me when words stopped
and pain spoke through hiccupped tears.
It used to be the place
where I felt the most alone
until I found You.

You found me
in this place where it feels safe to bleed,
where wolves have no access
to the wounded sheep.

Prayer has become my lifeline,
knees surrendered completely.
I can't survive without You.

If I breathe but not for You, what's the use?
If I love but don't love You, what's the use?
If I speak but don't know You, what's the use?

This is the place where
my broken pieces have use—
in the house of my Father,
in the hands of the Potter,
my refuge.

Divorce

Mornings were always split
between the weekends of the month.
The only thing that felt consistent
was the café con leche in my mug.

Mornings at Mom's began with
Tibetan throat singing CDs
that always made my heart feel heavy.
She said they were supposed to
cleanse the bad energy.

At Papi's house, the sun rose
to the sound of Joel Osteen's voice on TV
preaching about faith and positivity.

The drives between
house and home
never became easier.

I always tried to sleep through them
to make the distance feel shorter.
I became friends with the bench
in the back of my father's pickup truck.

It held my back as I hid from the streetlights.
I would peek my eyes through the window
every few minutes to check
which landmark we were by:

the Sports Hotel,
the highway curve,
the Christmas store,
the Booby Trap,
the Pepsi factory,
the movie theater,
and finally, the light off my exit.

The weekends always ended
with a slow hug
and a walk to my front door.
My father hated those goodbyes;
I could feel it
in the way he tried
not to look at
the home he painted,
the door he hinged,
the walls he built.

Somehow,
it was my home now and not his.
He had to stay out,
and I was locked in.

Forty-six returned to its original state.
I felt my chromosomes divide
as those papers were signed,
each keeping their half of the contract.

From a young age,
my hands got used to
the weight of paper.

Each month,
my father slipped me
a small rectangular check
with numbers that looked like hieroglyphs
dedicated to my mom.

I could feel the thickness
of my father's resentment
from the pressed ink of his signature
that almost pierced through the paper.

I was careful with them—
carried them with the certainty
that my mom would receive them
as he paid for what was rightfully his.

It was hard for me to grasp.

Did Daddy have to pay to be mine?
Why did he knock now?
Why did he have to ask to come in?

This was his home—
the one he bled for,
the one he watered—
and now I was supposed to grow in it
without him.

I thank God my dad never left my life.
He fought day and night
to remind me he was still by my side.

But this flower—
this flower was trying to take root
while planted in two different pots
and being asked to bloom.

Miami's weather
never made sense with the seasons;
rain came down during each quarter.

Summer cried,
waiting for the sun to rise;
sometimes it would
take revenge with a hurricane,
and it rained.

Autumn was silenced in suspense;
the leaves didn't have
the audacity to change color,
and it rained.

Winter, winters made me sweat.
Holiday agendas made me nauseous.
At least Santa left double the presents,
but it rained.

Spring meant the ciruelas
my daddy and I used to pick were ripe,
but it rained.

Until my heart grew cloudy
like a summer's day,
autumn conceived storms in me,
winter made me cold,
and I couldn't spring out of it.

I started to breathe differently.
I remember my kindergarten
and second-grade teachers' names.
I could even picture their faces,
but first grade is opaque.

I started to act out.
My brother and I were like two gremlins
determined to make being
a single mother a living hell.

Mornings used to be Papi's job
since Mom worked the morning show,
so if the nannies gave up,
maybe Papi would come home,
but time proved this desire had no hope.

Even now,
I wish Papi could come home.

Glory

My testimony includes the areas
I've been set free from.
If I'm ashamed of from where I came,
how can anyone else experience freedom?

If I only testify of the
good things in life,
does God have the spotlight,
or am I the one being glorified?

Curiosity

Marriage and kids
were always part of my vision
until my freshman year
when I realized I loved this boy
with a simple heart, and he loved me.
I was so excited I told my family,
and when I told my cousin,
he listened while
he took advantage of me.

And all the love I had in my heart
for this dreamy boy
and our dreamy life
came rushing out of me
all at the same time.

My classmates started
asking me if I was gay,
like they saw something in me
that I discovered late.

I found a place in my mind
where I could hide.
I called it Curiosity,
and she called me special.

In a heartbeat,
all of my dreams collapsed
because finally
someone understood me.

I didn't have to explain
what it felt like to be
abused by your own blood,
by the people you trust—
she got me.

And just like that,
I gave up what I wanted most,
what I'd always dreamt of,
to protect myself
from what was done to me.

And I loved it,
until I saw the way
sin produced death in me.

Curiosity kills …

To Learn to Love

Fragments of a heart once shattered
surrendered at the edge of Your altar.
I came to You on my knees,
bleeding,
swallowing my pride,
afraid to admit
what I had to leave behind
were the same thorns
You were trying to remove from my spine.

I used to think love was blind,
that I was supposed to
turn off the lights and fall
from the sensation on my fingertips
or the ecstasy of skin on skin.

My mentality gave me
the freedom to justify my sin.
Not only did I conform
and eventually stop trusting men
but I allowed hate to distort
what love actually meant.

I thought it was something that
crept into your heart as eyes met
or in an instance of burning passion
between two lovers.

The lines between
love and infatuation
became discolored.

The sin committed against me
became the source of the sin
I put into action.

Surrendering was the opposite
of my innate fabrication,
and Christ was a man
I didn't know how to submit to.

I didn't know You were the one
knocking on my door,
trying to set me free.

The devil had me convinced
as he slid the handcuffs on my wrists
that You were the one who wanted me captive.

When I was ten,
I fractured my femur
and had to learn how to walk again.
I'm discovering this process
isn't that different.

I have a cast on my heart
not because it's hardened
but because it's healing.

I was like the woman
with the perpetual bleeding;
my heart was leaking,
but the veil over my eyes kept me blind.

It wasn't love that was disguised;
the distortion was in my mind.
So when Jesus crossed my path,
I didn't reach for His robe
but ran from His wrath.

Deception slithered its way
into my conscience;
with my own hands,
I brought destruction.

I hadn't realized
I was preparing my own crucifixion.
As I stepped back to look at what I'd done,
I saw Him hanging there
with my nails in His hands, the Son.
He found it fit to pay the price
that I was guilty of.

He performed the most
scandalous act of love
greater than
Romeo and Juliet,
Jack and Rose.
He rose from the grave
that was supposed to say my name.
He went on a relentless pursuit
to reunite me with You.

Holy Spirit,
You are my comforter;
Son,
my best friend;
Father,
my home;
the family I am now a part of.

I was bought by the blood.
Slowly, the fragments of this heart
will be sewn back together.

With broken bones
and a fragmented soul,
I place myself in Your hands,
not afraid of the future
but confident in what lies ahead,
and just as I did when I was ten,
I will learn to love again.

I will not run before my time.
I will crawl to You.
With that smile
and glimmer in Your eyes,
I will follow You.
I will trust You,
the Man and Head of my life.
As I've committed myself to You,
You've become my Husband
and I, Your wife.

You accepted me as I am,
washed my feet with Your very hands.
You came down from Your throne
to ask me to come home.

I'm sorry I ever ran from You,
but I'm so grateful You ran after me.
I was so empty before You.
Now, You've satisfied every craving.

My only desire
is to be in Your presence.
So strip me down;
remove all that separates me from You.
I won't flinch.
I won't move.
Now it is my turn
to pursue You.

Sisterhood

Ponytails,
I mastered them,
considering it was the only hairstyle
I knew how to do.
I made sure it was perfect,
slick.

Things I always wondered about,
girls who had sisters knew how:
fishtail braids and curling wands.
I twirled my ponytail and put it in a bun.

I always longed to feel safe with a sister.
Somehow I missed her,
like if I knew I was meant to have one
but missed out.

Sometimes I grieve
when I see pictures of sisters smiling
because I want to know what it feels like
to have a sister to stay up with at night,
to look out for me when I cry,
to call when I have bullies to fistfight.

Maybe that's why
I consider friendships to be so deep,
because for me,
it's the closest thing
to sisterhood.

Femininity

I used to see the Sunday dresses
longer than I'd ever thought I'd wear,
space between,
I felt the breeze,
I could feel the air,
I just never thought I could compare.

Victoria Secret models
walk down the runway
with their long plush hair,
waist small like mine,
limbs long like mine,
but I thought mine
I just had to hide.

Bodies like mine are idolized
and trash talked on sidewalks.
I thought being *woman* meant
I was supposed to have more curves
that bounced hopscotch across the playground.

Ears pierced, I only wore studs.
I broke little boys' ankles under hoops.
My hair was thick brown, curly loops.
Voice too bold, or so I was told.

Femininity.
I just couldn't find the fem in me.

My soul was robed in clothes
baggy enough to disguise my insecurities
but not thick enough
to stop the light from finding me.
My issue was
His word felt too good to be true.

If it was true
that He created
the heavens,
moons, and stars,
birds and bees,
Adam and Eve,
and everything in between.

If it was true
that there was someone separated,
one man He created
with a hole in his ribs
and a scar on his flesh
that was the evidence of God's design,
then how come my shoulders
feel bolder than a man's spine?
Why did my heart
feel too rigid to embrace?
Why did submission,
an institution designed for my protection,
feel like suppression?

My heart desired to love,
but it was in a wicked affair
with the shadows of my past.

I searched long and hard
to find what was missing.
I gathered all the debris
from the words spoken against me
or the ones people failed to say,
from every moment
of misplaced affection
and acceptance.

I searched the basketball courts
I was cheered on
and the cheer teams
I was booed off.
I tried building myself *woman*
out of cardboard boxes
I used to hide in.

Marriage and motherhood felt like Goliaths
I was unprepared to conquer.
I had all the stones in my hand,
but I was too small for the armor.

If I felt inadequate as a woman,
how could I
teach my baby girl
her curls are beautiful,
her face doesn't need a mask to hide behind,
her smile shines even if she has a few crooked teeth,
her body is a sacred temple never to be trespassed,
her heart should be cherished and protected,
her voice isn't too loud,
but it's a trumpet that will resound
in her generation?

The truth is
I was a woman walking dead
with a graveyard of truths.

Divorce taught me the woman was the head,
and the man had to submit.
Seeing my father every other weekend
turned split personalities into a trend.
Abuse broke down any wholeness I had left,
and drugs drowned out the silence of death.

Femininity was too hard to put on.

Woman,
I thought,
if only they knew
how hard it is
to be woman.

I grew to believe my femininity
was synonymous with fragility.

I traded my dresses for pants.
I hid the sight of my curves
so they wouldn't be confused for weakness.
I puffed out my chest and lowered my voice
so there was no hint of innocence left to rob.
I did all I could to deflect the attention of men
and ended up attracting the same sex.

I made an idol for myself
of what I thought men should be,
thinking I could do it better.

I sacrificed my identity
at the feet of momentary security,
thinking I could heal myself
by loving someone else.

Love is not love
when it's not
the holy love
God loves us with.

He did not make a mistake
when He made me *woman*.

He did not make a mistake
when He made you *man*.

Identity and sexuality are not things
we can redefine or invent;
all else is pretend and coveted
from His original intent.

Femininity and masculinity
are not social constructs.
The devil has just tried to distort
what God already defined as good.

We put coverings on ourselves
in attempts to hide our shame,
as if God can't see
through the leaves He made,
through the flesh He formed,
through the heart He loved into existence.

His perfect love
cast out all my fear.
His word was true.
He loved me enough
to make sure my heart knew love too.

So I opened the doors to my heart,
let Him into every closet
and flipped every mattress,
there wasn't an ounce of me I kept hidden.

I wanted to be known intimately.
I wanted Him to see into me.
It didn't come easily—
starting to live in the image,
in the vision
of the God that designed me.

He defines me:
fearfully and wonderfully made.

I am alabaster clay
crafted in the palm of His hands,
curved by the breath on His lips,
filled by the waters that run deep,
washed by the blood that freed me.

My identity won't be defined by society
or bound by my anxieties.
My beauty flows from His joy,
my every inch is evidence of His fingerprints.

Femininity is not the clothes you wear.
It is not the makeup on your face.

You are powerful,
not because of your gender,
simply because of the image
in which you were made.

Femininity is found in your character
not just your curves,
in your morality and integrity
not just your nudity or modesty,
in your fear of the Lord and humility,
in your love for the Father.

Femininity looks like the Church—
giving Herself only to Him,
carrying His children,
preparing them for purpose,
and adorning them for His return.

It was You …
It was Your hand
that carved me out of dust,
formed me in my mother's womb,
called me by my name.
the apple of His eye;
His bride.
Woman.

He is the great I Am.
As long as He comes first,
everything I am is enough.

You

I met you after the first autumn sunrise,
my feet still burning
from the scorching summer sand,
my hair wild and yet perfectly tamed.

I saw you
but didn't draw close,
assuming you were another ghost
I'd fantasized in the desert heat.

I watched you for a few weeks,
remained motionless to see
if you would take what you needed and leave.

I was reluctant to look in your direction,
afraid your reflection would reveal
the completion of a million promises.

I approached you with caution.

It has always been just the Lion and a girl,
roaming through the wild,
slaying every Goliath on our own.
I grew accustomed to being alone
until you came.

You pursued me with patience,
allowing my heart to breathe and grieve
all at the same time.

Breathing in the beauty of love
and breathing out the reality
that I would never be alone
in this garden again.

Falling for you was
as easy as autumn leaves
retiring after a fruitful summer.

Although I'd prefer to say
I walked into love with you,
it was no accident.

Therefore, I cannot blame
the fleeting nature of my heart
when it tells me that
running is as easy as falling.

Rather, I will stand and remember
the reason I walked down the aisle to "I do."
Falling means my God would have dropped me,
but He held on tightly to my heart
when He led me to you.

Walking into love with you
gave me the opportunity
to stand in love with you.

Friendly Fire

Friendly fire revealed that you are
an iron sent to sand the triggers off my back.

I have debris in places where proximity
won't allow me to see,
like the plank in my eye.

In intimacy, we have the gift of healing.
This is the most vulnerable I have ever been,
but you are safe,
not because you are perfect,
but because there is purpose in our midst.

Loving you challenged me
to surrender my life a second time
and every day.

I leave my gun in its case
and pick up my sword.
This is a patient war
with one enemy,
and you are not him.

Red Flags

If he asks for your body
before he asks for your hand,
he is not the one.

If he asks you to come to his place
before he asks to meet your parents,
he is not the one.

If he offers you attention
without protection,
he is not the one.

The right man
leads you into purity
not promiscuity.

The right man will pursue you
not prey on you;
pray about you
with no added pressure.

When a man finds a wife,
he has found a good thing.

This is what makes the difference
between a boy and a man.

A man becomes your husband;
a boy plays house.

Appetite

Sexual purity looks more like
managing your appetite
than controlling what appeals to you.

You can't control what catches your eye,
but you can control what you eat.

What attracts you
is not who you are.

Surfaced

So many parts of me
were buried beneath
people pleasing
and fawning.

So welcome,
or welcome back.

Love

Until you've encountered
the love of God,
you have not
known love at all.

Unfinished

I healed,
I am healing,
and I will be healed.

I am saved,
I am being saved,
and I will be saved.

Yesterday,
today,
and tomorrow.

Innocent

My therapist prompted me
to ask the little girl in me
what her favorite color is,
to which she responded,

"Pink."

I wasn't surprised,
but at the same time,
I cried
because I knew
at some point in time
pink didn't feel safe anymore.

Somewhere between that little girl
and who I am today
black and red
became my defense.

Pink was naïve.
Pink did a poor job
of protecting me.

Red and black
came in when I was fifteen
to protect me from
what my innocence
failed to see.

Abuse has a way of changing
your favorite color
from pink to red,
your conscience
from white to black.

Innocence,
from my perspective,
no longer belonged to me.

And yet, the word says
He clothes me in robes of righteousness,
my sins are thrown into the depths of the ocean,
nothing created in heaven or on earth
can separate me from His love.

So, if He sees me innocent,
pink can still be my favorite color.

THE
DISCOVERY

Birth

Taking ownership of my birth
healed the dissociation
I had long lived in.

Birth led me
to hear my body,
and my body was screaming,
begging to be heard.

Birth led me
to trust my body
after years of feeling
betrayed by my own skin.

Redemption came
in the form of surrender.
Pregnancy and birth
pressed me
to trust myself again.

Priorities

My daughter is my priority,
and in seconds,
moments,
in a minute
I realized
I am willing to sacrifice
every comfort zone,
every defense mechanism,
every coping strategy,
any relationship,
any opportunity
that does not prioritize
her well-being,
and that meant
prioritizing my own.

I am your mother,
so I will go first.
I'll lead you
not by my words
but by the steps
I leave in the sand.
I'll teach you
not by my words
but by my presence.
You'll never have to question
why I wasn't present;
I'll be there.

I am your mother.

Home will always be
the memories we've made,
the words we've shared,
and the songs we've sung.

I'll teach you,
time after time,
who you are
when you forget.

You are
loved,
adored,
chosen,
covered,
promised,
cherished,
important,
consecrated,
whole.

You are our priority,
but you were His first.

Eden

In the garden,
we can see that
Man's infatuation
with creation
will always
lead us away
from the love
of our Creator.

Honor

The empowerment of women
does not require
the degradation of men.

The empowerment of women
requires
the edification of men.

Women and men alike are
broken down by
our own definitions of good and evil.

When women honor men
and men honor women,
we are able to honor the parts of us
that make us different.

Nature

Pain is a signal in the body
that something is going wrong
or that a piece of you is broken.
I am familiar with the sensation.

I trust the intensity of labor
was crafted by a God
who is gracious enough
to cloth me in strength.

If pain were to come,
I trusted my body
would know the difference between
what it needs and when it needs help.

As contractions came slowly,
like waves on a beach
during a midnight sky,
I sat by and waited.

Knowing that night
inevitably brings a sunrise,
I trusted my body
would inevitably give light.

I wasn't afraid
of the intensity of the waves;
my body was doing exactly
what it was built to do.

With power and pressure,
the same way the wind blows over the waves
and the waters rush under the currents,
my body bore down.

Unmedicated,
without interference,
after three nights and three days
at our own pace,
my daughter came.

Some say it's courageous,
but I believe it is our nature.
I wish more women knew
birth belongs to you.

New

Allow me to reintroduce myself,
because in every season
there is a new aspect of God
I am seeing,
and a new version of me
I am meeting.

Come Home

The foundation of our identity
rests upon the realization that
we are daughters
of the Most High King
with direct access to Him.
Imagine what it feels like
to come home.

Born

Healing from trauma
while your daughter
lays asleep on your chest
is no easy task.

It is recognizing the knives
that have inflicted pain
with the brutal awareness
that they can cut her, too,
and praying they never do.

It's knowing the statistics
you fell into,
what you've lived through,
and praying that she never does.

And that if she does,
you have the strength
to carry her through.

I didn't expect
being a mother
to set aflame
every painful memory
as it has.

I thought love would come,
and I'd forget.
On the contrary,
love came and I became enraged.
Hyper aware.
She was born,
and I transformed
into a bear in the wilderness,
ready to tear down any threat
that comes near her.

Knuckles

Touch my kids,
and you'll
catch these fists.
Sorry,
my ghetto
slipped.

Scarlet

Homosexuality is not
the scarlet letter sin.

It is not the sin that is too strong
or too engraved in the flesh
to be washed by the blood of Jesus.

It's not a letter worn
on the chest with shame
for those that have been set free
or have prayed to be.

It's not the sin
that is too powerful
for repentance.

Homosexuality, however,
is a sin, and this is good news.

This good news means
the blood of Jesus,
scarlet red,
still has the power to conquer
sin and death
in you.

This good news means
the desire you feel in your body
to do everything against
what God designed for you
still has the ability to be submitted
to a holy and righteous God.

Relationship with Jesus
will always call you
into holiness
and out of sin.

Anything that says otherwise
is counterfeit.

This is good news
because the blood of Jesus,
scarlet red,
still has the power
to save you.

He saved me.

Break

Allow God to break down
the walls of your heart.
It might hurt, but you'll heal,

and you'll see clear as day.

The Work of a Mother

The work of a mother is hard,
it is slow, and it is fleeting.
Every moment is a different mission,
and every day is repetitious.

The mundane is my workman's table.
The work of now and eternity.

Motherhood is an invitation
into the Potter's house.

The love that you give
or the love you withhold
has the power to harm or mold
the clay you hold.

The work of a mother
is allowing His hands
to use you as a sculpting tool,
not knowing how the vase will turn out
but knowing He has begun the work
and that work starts with you.

In the mundane,
the day to day,
every diaper change,
every bubble bath,
every lullaby,
every sleepless night.

The work of a mother
can't be seen by accolades,
but it can be felt
in the way her children praise her,
in the way they trust her,
in the way they call her name.

The work of a mother
is the work of building a home
in the child's heart and
teaching the child
how to dwell in it,
how to rest in it.

Hardly can you see the work of a mother
because she has usually cleaned it up
by the time you come home.

So be grateful for the food on the plate
that she rushed to make.
Be thankful for the quiet while you rest,
she stayed up to give the baby breast.
Be aware of the way she yawns
because exhaustion has become part of the work.
It is the forest she fights through daily
to make sure her baby is well taken care of.

Sweet Momma,
I hope you know
you're valuable.
You're doing a great job,
even when you feel unseen.
You are doing kingdom work
in raising your babies.
Hold them extra tight.
Let them see you
pray while you sweep,
come back together
after you weep,
because every part of you
is what your baby needs.

Daughter

Keep your heart tender, my dear,
even when hurt tries
with all its might to harden it.

A tender heart
will set you apart
and keep you
in the will of God.

Never let this world
suffocate the fire in your belly.
Maintain the curiosity in your eyes
and the wonder to observe details.

My prayer is that joy
never leaves your heart,
faith never loses its spark,
and hope endures to the end.

Be wise and humble,
cherish your friends,
honor your family,
and love deeply.

Joy,
what a joy it is
to love you.

Hindsight

If I would have known
the way love would come
and sweep me up
one day,

I would not have
given myself over
to youthful lusts.

I would have preserved
my memory from knowing
other lovers' names.

I would have preserved my heart
from becoming one with people
I was not in covenant with.

If I would have known
what I know today,
I would have had the hope
to wait.

Love is worth the wait.

Disconnect

When femininity is disconnected
from Christianity,
our identity is disconnected
from our Maker.

Dissociation may play a role
since defense mechanisms
can tend to control
the way we operate.

We begin to unplug everything
that is a threat to our safety,
even if it's at the cost
of our God-given identity.

Self-preservation
can become our self-destruction
when it is divorced
from biblical truth.

This generation's identity
lacks a cross.
The cross that crucified sin
and called us to be crucified with Him.

When we disconnect
our ears from culture
and connect our hearts to the word,
our identity can be restored.

Exploit

Women have fallen victim
to a society that pays for their nudity,
suppresses their fertility,
and monetizes childbearing
while simultaneously
becoming the type of women
that can conform successfully
to a society that hates them.

Industrialized exploitation.

Rebel

Feminism is a failed attempt
to rebel against captivity.
Unaware of the true enemy,
the feminist
stripped herself down,
asked for money in return,
decided never to be a wife,
and not to carry life in her womb.

Desiring liberation,
she imprisoned herself.
Fighting to be heard,
she isolated herself,
unknowingly becoming exactly
what was expected of her.

A rebel against the Lord,
sacrificing her true liberty—
to have eternal salvation
and a soul that is free.

If you're going to rebel,
rebel against the works of the enemy.

You're Safe

Maybe, just maybe
if you felt safe,
if the survival mode
you've been in
could step away,
you'd find
that the person
you've had to become
to protect yourself
is not who you actually
want to be,
and maybe, just maybe
if you had safety,
you'd flourish
into the woman
you were
designed
to be.

Community

I want to live in a world
where women are not afraid
to ask other women
for help,
for advice,
for resources,
for love,
for compassion,
for sympathy,
for wisdom,
for a hug,
for guidance,
for good counsel,
for strength,
for inspiration.

I want to see the walls of contention
between generations fall
and the battlefield of competition
turn into training grounds.

Women need women.

Coffee Shop

A young woman feels alone,
and an older woman feels without purpose,
and the two walk by each other
without a word said,
even with a glance of judgment.

Take a second,
sit down,
share a cup of coffee.

Beauty

When you look in the mirror
and search your reflection for flaws,
calculating the cost to perfect them all,
thinking of a way to look younger,
lose more weight,
put on more muscle,
change your hair color,
desiring to fit into the mold
that media and modern medicine
have defined as beautiful,
remember that ...

pregnancy is beautiful,
aging is beautiful,
wrinkles are beautiful,
gray hairs are beautiful,
stretch marks are beautiful.

Beauty is not
youth or the elasticity of your skin.
Beauty is
the evidence that you have lived.

Ancestry

I found out I was pregnant
a few weeks after
my grandmother passed away.
It's safe to say, at that moment,
I became brutally aware of the way
grief and joy, life and death,
are not foes but friends

As one incredibly courageous woman,
who left her country so that the women
that came after her could give birth
in a land that offers better opportunities,
left this earth and went homebound to heaven,
I became fiercely aware that
I'm not the first woman,
I'm not the first daughter,
I'm not the first mother
that has had to cross the terrain
of becoming a parent
and seeing parents fade.

Having my daughter in a time
where I didn't have my grandmother
made me aware of how essential
the passing on of our history is,
like a baton in the hands of the next runner,
like the tools on the belt of a carpenter,
history is for our self-esteem and destiny.

In a time where I'm raising my daughter
I wish I could ask my grandmother
what it was like to be raised by her mother,
what it was like to raise my mother,
and what it was like to help my mother raise me,
what she would do differently.

This is the importance of ancestry—
it lets us know we're not alone,
it gives us a path for where we want to go
or where we don't,
and it lets us know we're not the first ones,
generations have gone before us.

I know from the way
my mother smiles at me
that my grandmother
would have been proud
of the woman I've become.

Take It Back

My children will learn about birth
in our home, not a hospital.
My children will learn about marriage
in our home, not a court hearing.
My children will learn about identity
in our home, not on television.
My children will learn about feelings
in our home, not in therapy.
My daughters will learn about femininity
in our home, not on social media.
My children will learn their worth
in our home, not on the streets.
My children will learn about God
in our home, not only from pulpits.
That's how we take it back—

We stop allowing the village
to raise our children,
and we bring them home.

Good

The first time
God looked at creation
and said that it was not good
was when He looked
at all He had made
and saw that
Woman wasn't in it.

When Eve ate the fruit
that sewed sin
into the fabric of humanity,
God had already planted
the seed of salvation
in her womb.

God chose the womb
of a woman
to carry,
to create,
to hold
the Savior of the world.

He chose to form woman,
knowing we'd be fallen
and knowing He would
restore us Himself.

Found

I found it when I stopped
trying to be provider and priest
and gave myself to homemaking.

I found it in the way
my body had space
for two sets of lungs
and two heartbeats.

I found it in therapy,
a little girl terrified to come out,
finally confident enough
to stand on her own two feet
and speak.

I found it in the way
my daughter looks at me
and knows I'm her mother.
The way she cries for comfort,
only relieved by my arms.

Nurturing didn't feel foreign.
It felt like I was finally able to come home.
Loving my daughter taught me
to love the little girl in me.

I found it nestled within my bones
and sown into the fabric of my being.

Femininity
was not something to put on
but settle into.

Femininity
always belonged to me,
just took me some time
to find it.

Acknowledgments

Thank you to every woman
who lent me their courage,
poured into my life,
and believed in me.

I completed this book with
you all in my heart.
Thank you for pushing me.
Thank you for hearing me.
Thank you for covering me.
Thank you for loving me.

I pray that if you've seen yourself in
the words I've written, you also see
you're not alone and there are
women that are standing with you.

About the Author

Bianca Irene was raised with her two brothers in the heart of Miami by her parents that work in television. She has always had a heart for communication and art, having studied photography and graphic design. Bianca has been writing poetry for over a decade, performing her Spoken Word poetry throughout Miami and New York. Bianca became a born again Christian at the age of 18 years old and is passionate about telling the world about Jesus' saving grace. At the age of 21, she married her husband Sebastian Corriero who is a musician and songwriter. She is the owner of a Christian clothing line, Oil Clothing, Co. After giving birth to her firstborn, Bianca has written and published her first book Femininity.

To connect with Bianca Irene you may email her at biancairenewrites@gmail.com or follow her on Instagram @bianca_irene

Printed in the United States
by Baker & Taylor Publisher Services